THE EMOTES BIG BOOK OF FEELINGS

By Matt Casper, MFT and Ted Dorsey

Evergrow Ltd.
Hong Kong - Los Angeles
www.Emotes.com

THERE ARE SO MANY FEELINGS TO FEEL! IN FACT, THERE ARE AS MANY FEELINGS AS THERE ARE EMOTES!

CAN YOU FIND WHICH EMOTE YOU FEEL LIKE TODAY?

ABASH
FEELS EMBARRASSED.
IT'S OKAY
IF YOU MAKE A MISTAKE.
NOBODY'S PERFECT!

ABASH
(THE EMBARRASSED)

ONE WAY TO SHOW
LOVE IS TO TAKE
CARE OF YOUR FRIENDS.
THANKS FOR THE LOVE, AMORE!

AMORE
(THE LOVING)

BOOM FEELS ANGRY!
TAKE A DEEP BREATH, BOOM!
COUNT TO 10!

BOOM
(THE ANGRY)

PAINTING MAKES BUBBA FEEL **HAPPY.**

WHAT MAKES YOU FEEL **HAPPY?**

BUBBA
(THE HAPPY)

WHEN CANT CANNOT DO SOMETHING, CANT FEELS FRUSTRATED.

CANT
(THE FRUSTRATED)
02

EMOTIA SCHOOL
LAST NIGHT
DRAIN STAYED UP
WAY TOO LATE.
THIS MORNING
DRAIN FEELS VERY TIRED.

DRAIN
(THE TIRED)

HEY GRUMP!
WHY ARE YOU FEELING
GRUMPY?
DID YOU SKIP BREAKFAST?
DID YOU STUB YOUR BIG TOE?

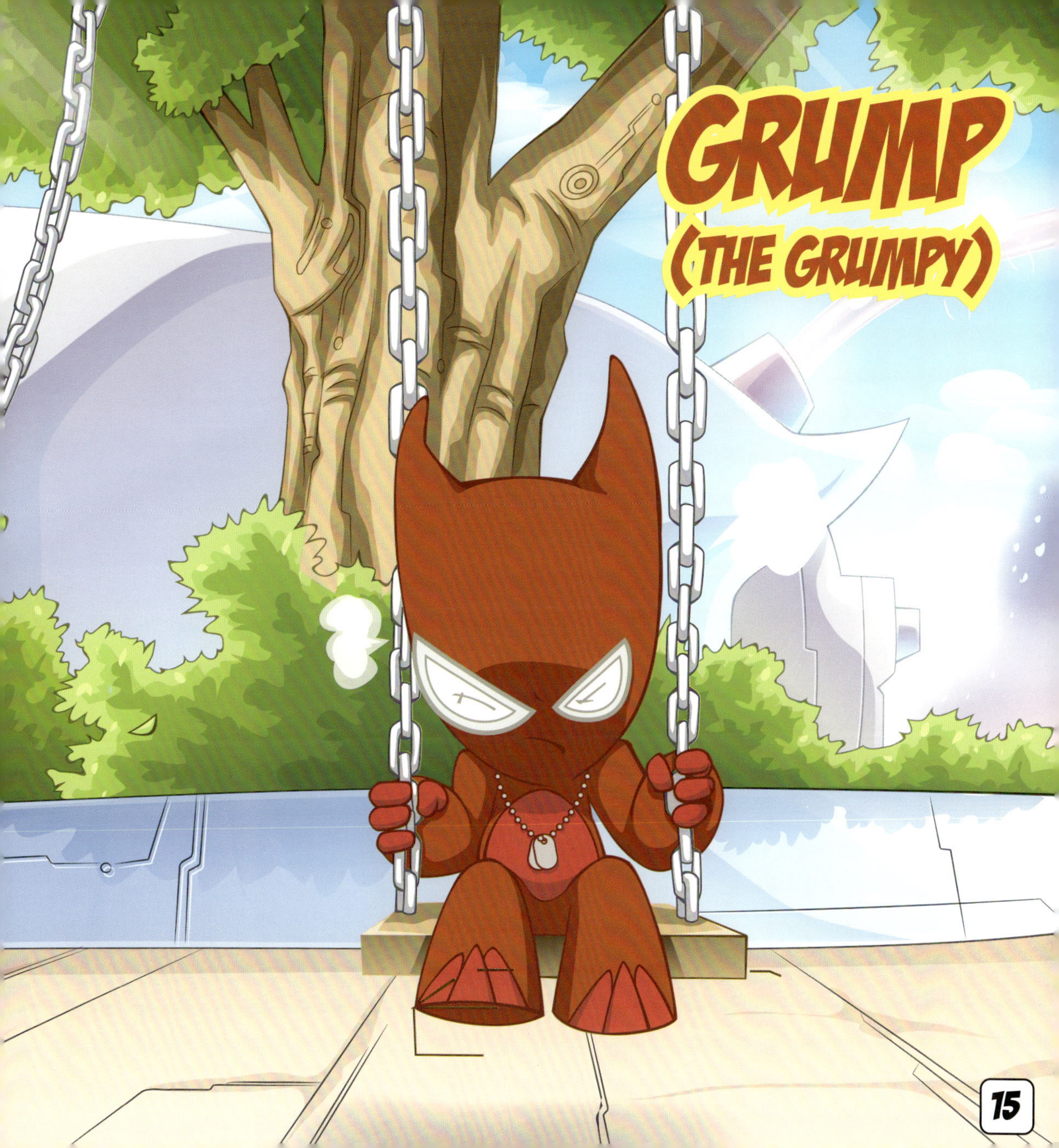
GRUMP
(THE GRUMPY)

WHEN HYPE FEELS FRISKY
HYPE HAS A HARD TIME SITTING STILL.
SLOW DOWN HYPE!

HYPE
(THE FRISKY)

GROSS!
WHEN ICK SEES
SLIMY-CREEPY-CRAWLIES
ICK FEELS DISGUSTED.
DO YOU?

ICK
(THE DISGUSTED)

WHEN IMP FEELS PLAYFUL,
IMP PLAYS PRANKS AND TELLS JOKES.
IT'S OKAY TO JOKE AND PLAY...
JUST PLAY IT SAFE!

IMP
(THE PLAYFUL)

IT'S JOI'S BIRTHDAY.
JOI FEELS VERY EXCITED!
HAPPY BIRTHDAY JOI!

Happy
Birthday
JOI
(THE EXCITED)

JUMPI FEELS SCARED.
WHEN YOU FEEL SCARED,
TELL SOMEBODY!

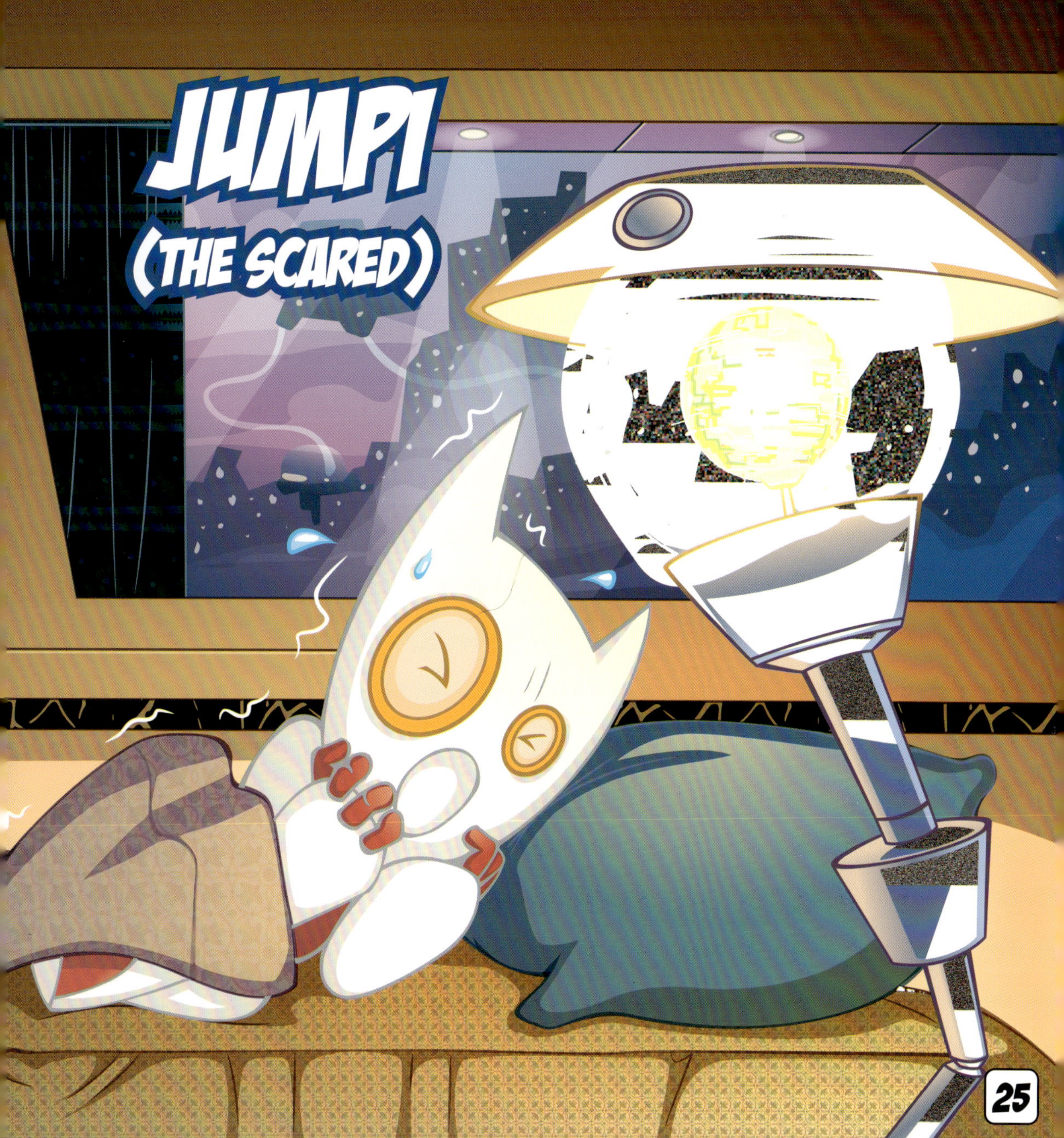
JUMPI
(THE SCARED)

"MINE! MINE! MINE!"
MINE FEELS ENVIOUS.
MINE WANTS EVERYTHING.
BE THANKFUL FOR WHAT YOU HAVE!
(YOU HAVE GOOD THINGS TOO!)

MINE
(THE ENVIOUS)

MIXY FEELS **CONFUSED!**

MIXY DOESN'T KNOW WHICH WAY TO GO. DO YOU?

TALK TO A GROWN UP... THAT'S A GOOD THING TO DO!

MIXY
(THE CONFUSED)
Hospital

"NO! NO! NO!"
WHEN MULE FEELS STUBBORN, MULE ONLY SAYS "NO!"
HEY, MULE TRY SAYING "YES!"
IT MIGHT BE FUN!

MULE
(THE STUBBORN)

ODD FEELS WACKY!
THAT'S COOL!
BE PROUD! BE YOU!
EMOTES

ODD
(THE WACKY)

SAYING GOODBYE
MAKES SOB FEEL SAD.
EVERYONE FEELS SAD SOMETIMES.
IT'S TOTALLY OKAY TO CRY.

SOB
(THE SAD)

WHAT'S UP SOLO?
YOU LOOK LONELY.
MAYBE JOI WOULD LIKE TO PLAY.

SOLO
(THE LONELY)

WHEN SUPER FEELS
CONFIDENT
SUPER SAYS,
"I CAN DO ANYTHING
THAT I WANT TO DO!"

SUPER
(THE CONFIDENT)

WHEN WHY FEELS CURIOUS WHY ASKS MANY QUESTIONS.

"WHY IS THE SKY BLUE?"

"HOW DO AIRPLANES DO WHAT THEY DO?"

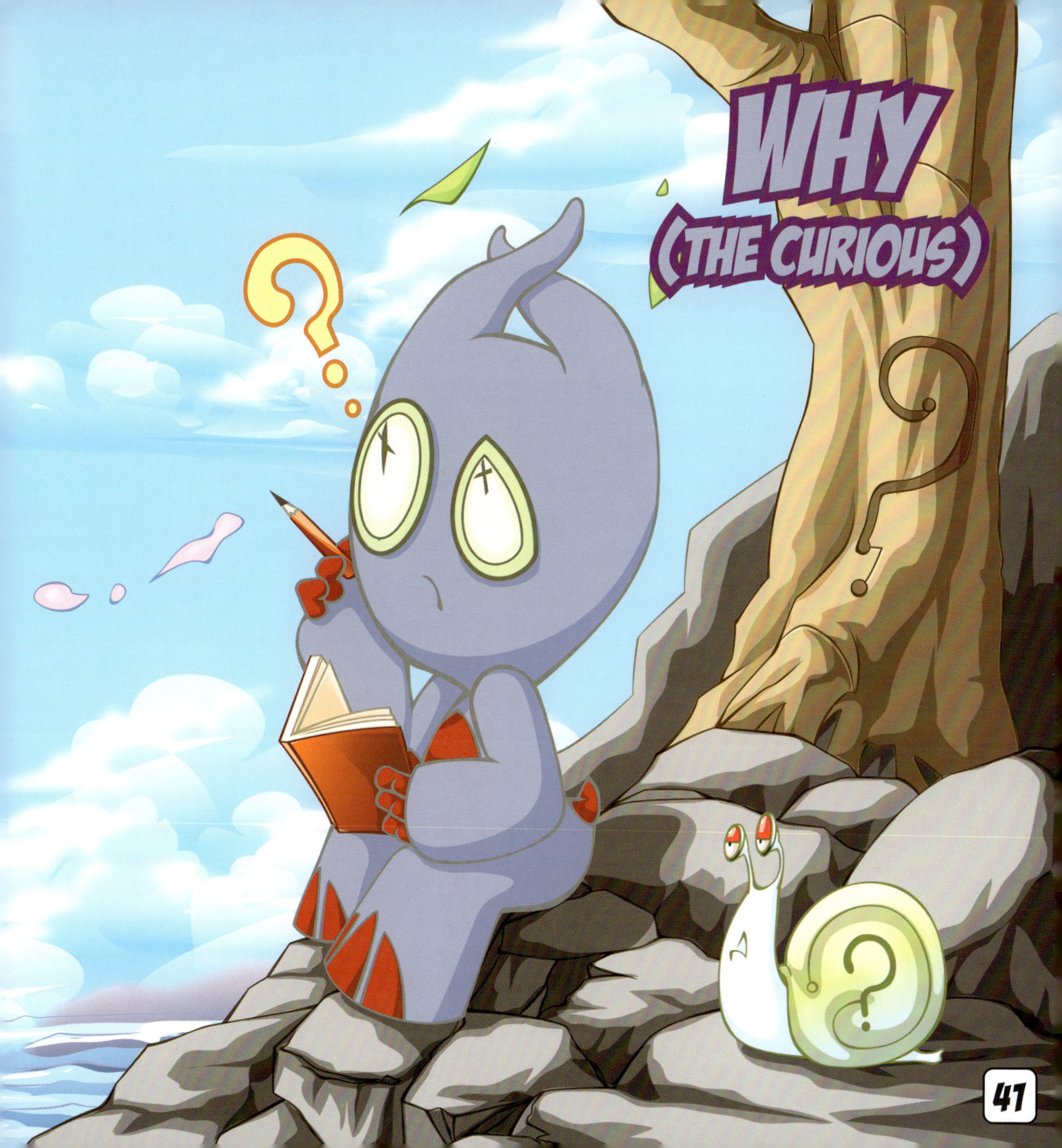
WHY
(THE CURIOUS)

"I THINK THE SUN WILL SHINE!"
WILL FEELS OPTIMISTIC.
WILL IS SURE THAT EVERYTHING WILL BE OKAY.

WILL
(THE OPTIMISTIC)

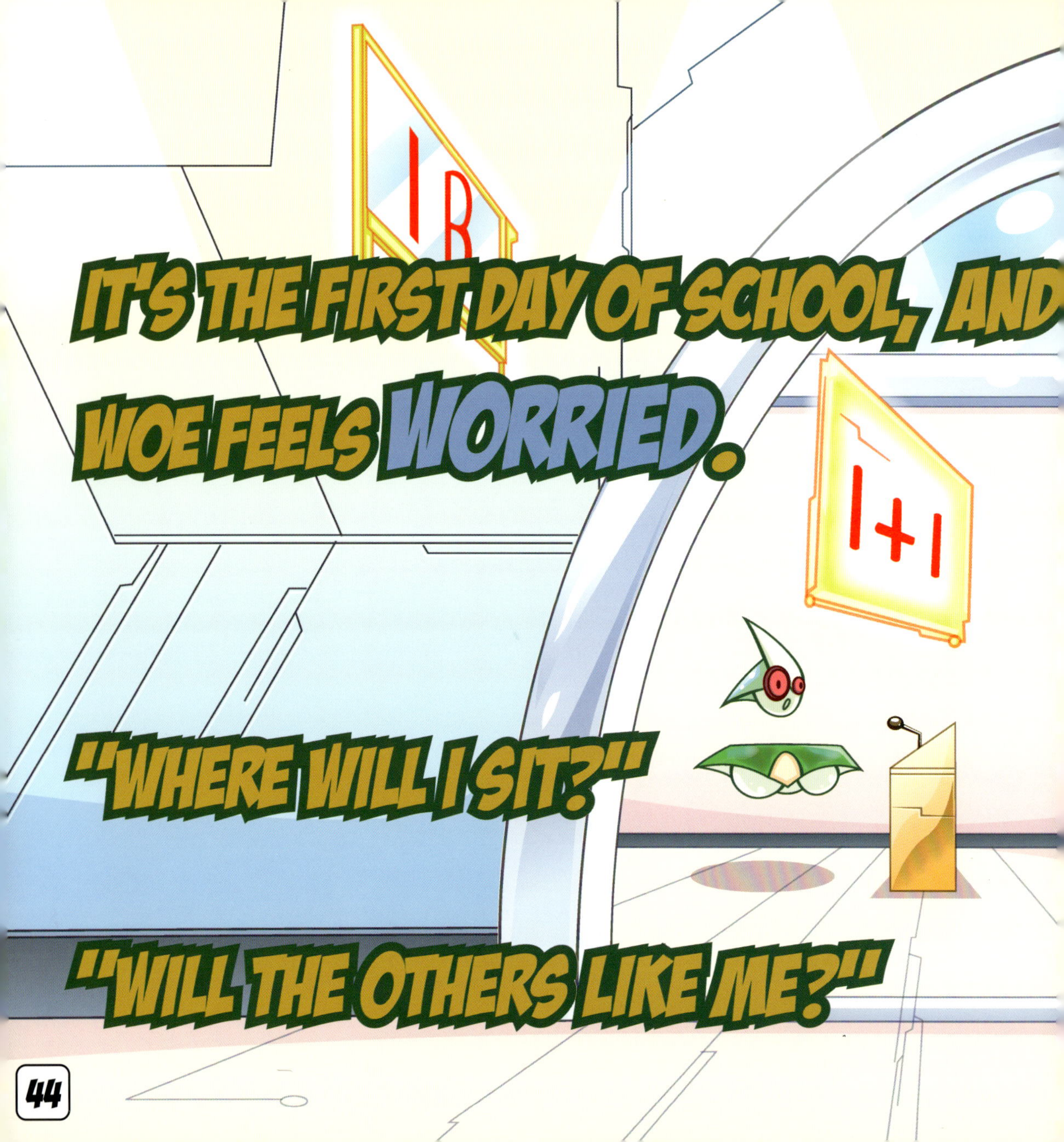
IT'S THE FIRST DAY OF SCHOOL, AND
WOE FEELS WORRIED.
"WHERE WILL I SIT?"
"WILL THE OTHERS LIKE ME?"
1B
1+1

WOE
(THE WORRIED)

WONT FEELS DOUBTFUL.

"I DOUBT MY FRIENDS WILL PICK ME TO PLAY", SAYS WONT.

WONT
(THE DOUBTFUL)

YAWNI FEELS **BORED.**

BEAT THE BOREDOM BLUES.

TRY SOMETHING NEW!

YAWNI
(THE BORED)

SO...

HOW ARE YOU FEELING TODAY?
02

ABOUT THE AUTHORS

Matt Casper, M.A. MFT. Matt is a licensed psychotherapist with a private practi in Los Angeles, California. He graduated cum laude from Duke University and has master's degree in marriage and family therapy.

Ted Dorsey is a writer and independent educator living in Los Angeles, Californ A graduate of Princeton University, he has written for the stage, film, and television.

ISBN 13: 978-988-19072-4-0

Printed in China